INVITING BLINDNESS

Other books by Bill Gaston

SHORT STORIES

Deep Cove Stories
North of Jesus' Beans

NOVELS

The Cameraman
Tall Lives
The Bella Combe Journal

INVITING BLINDNESS

by

BILL GASTON

oolichan books
LANTZVILLE, BRITISH COLUMBIA, CANADA
1995

Cover image "Shared Experience," by Ian Garrioch, used by permission of the artist.

Canadian Cataloguing in Publication Data

Gaston, Bill, 1953-
Inviting blindness

Poems.
ISBN 0-88982-145-3

I. Title.
PS8563.A76I58 1995   C811'.54   C95-910242-6
PR9199.3.G37I58 1995

The publisher gratefully acknowledges the financial assistance of the Canada Council.

Published by
Oolichan Books
P.O. Box 10
Lantzville, B.C.
Canada

Printed in Canada by
Hignell Printing, Ltd
Winnipeg, Manitoba

For Joan

Acknowledgements

Versions of some of these poems have appeared in *Poetry Canada Review, Waves, Event, Arc, Quarry, Prism International, Windhorse, Antigonish Review, Fiddlehead, Ariel, Wascana Review, Garden Varieties, Capilano Review,* and *Matrix.*

CONTENTS

I.

SEX IS RED

Housekeeping

—for D.

We eat first, then pause
to lace fingers across the table.
I see us entwined too
through belief in a human Spring.
Washing dishes
romantically, soothing egg from morning bowls, we
know the carnality of that.
Talk.
Destiny has become an easy word,
hopeful magic
that's probably false
but what lover won't pretend it?
I watch you
and see the skull behind your face,
lips clinging lively to bone that
will die as it is.
But we will make love when the dishes are done,
nerves in flesh on bones.
And I will find I can love it,
loving most the ornaments
of hair and smell and eyes.
But first I find your hand
under the dishwater:
a newness almost embarrassing.

And, dancing between,
a knife.
We discover again
Earth's sharp eye.

I send my birds out

Looking for you, I send my birds out
to take eaves in beak and lift the roofs
of houses in your rumoured neighbourhood.
It is my right: there were promises.
I send a flock of special chickens to slaughter.
They know who eats them, and where, and even why.
Can you blame me? You took my past
and without my past I cannot land.
Closing in, the hummingbird at your window
is a camera, the beat of its wings my heart.
I am not being pathetic.
As you will see:
You on the duck pond bench alone.
The swan that glides to foot so knowingly
will show, with ancient looping of neck,
the invitation
of half a human heart.

I always help her out with her language difficulties

She strains at explaining her bad mood and can't.
We fight, and on my rush out to the park I close the
door gently, a sneer. Walking, I think: that
mood of hers! Is it like *knives that leap out and surprise?*
Is it *a huge hole filled with birds?* Or *supermarket
purgatory, the shooting price of cheese, boredom? Fear
of breathing alone?* "Exactly!" she shouts from the porch
a block away, "It feels *like this! like this!*" I know
she points at me, I can feel her finger in the small of
my back, I know I have hold of that finger and am taking it
with me again, pulling it out of our anger, out the
door, to the park, and god knows when I will give it back.

The Challenge

We are drinking and the challenge
is to stand, embracing, until one of us finds
the right metaphor for our loving.
So, we hold on and think.
Always clever, I say, Surgery of the Rose
and you say no.
We stumble around the room, chest to chest,
refusing to quit, your muse descending in.
Your eyes are underwater bones.
I whisper Pandora's Smile
but you say nothing, you
hover in pain somewhere between our ribs.
At long last you hiss
Guernica
and even as I say What? I feel—the limbs
of lovers eternally kicking out, the abstract horse
rearing up, gut to gut, eyes and teeth
blind and gnashing.
So clear, as mindless as
primary colours splashed,
this war.
A Wonderful Guernica, you say again.
I have to nod. You win. We part for the couch.
The angle of your sitting is grotesque.
I know unless we love tonight,
to break the lines and close your eyes,
one more war will be lost.

Suddenly One Sunday

You, in pain again
from too much thinking
Here, I said, have some tea,
one herbal remedy dreamed up
by a lover from the hills
to give your mind time off

Stretching like a dog, then feigning sleep
on the bent couch,
you held the cooling cup
on the table
between your feet

Then—
within a smallest moment,
like music half-heard,
I saw you really trying

to die

Difference an Age Makes

Remembering how as kids
we'd talk about walking into those woods forever.
And almost did it too—
small creepings into the first line of trees,
each step muffling the city noise,
that vast poisoned father behind us
         —soon erased, quiet, then
         strangely missed—
our poison now the home we'd
run to wildly.

Yesterday, again,
we gathered enough for long trail days
and half packed the idea
of hanging around the woods forever;
that graceful father
too wise for us now, growing deadlier by the hour.
They scowl by night
these trees
given the gift of cool revenge.

We had time left, yet walked back faster
to our vast poisoned child
         —our city now—
the home we make
necessary.

Physics

People engage dumb as billiard balls or apples clicking off each other, bouncing, missing, falling, as the case may be. There appear to be laws about this.

A law called magnetism. It needs two surfaces that attract each other. For people, this surface is skin. Eyes put the final lock on things. It feels like a simple law. Much harder to understand is the law of one magnet letting go. The magnet that keeps pulling cannot understand the one that lets go, for it looks like lawlessness. A goddamn crime.

A law called momentum. It was years ago, maybe twenty, that you left me. My life smashed face-first against an irresistible object. Yet my love kept going, right through the wall, following you blindly. A part of me, I don't know the proportion, loved you after for a long time. Somewhere in my body, I still do. Everybody knows this momentum.

There are other laws. Gravity almost saw me a suicide. Inertia had me wasting a life in front of the TV or in dreams—though I could hardly recall your face anymore. And there was the peculiar velocity of my search for you, or someone like you, in bars. Friction made me dance like a maniac. Made me look at my watch to see how much time I had left.

But momentum is more interesting than velocity. Velocity, and the hairy damn friction that law says must come with it, needs a body and feels blind, like fever. Momentum doesn't need a body. Momentum is a comfy spirit that cruises along and doesn't like change. I think the spirit of momentum would be afraid of you now.

I remember when I first learned to skate. I mastered gravity and velocity enough to stop pushing and just glide, the wind roaring in my ears, hair whipping my neck. I had no destination. I could not stop in any case. And when I reached the end of the rink and smacked loud and final into the boards, something just kept going, fast, beyond a body, something that feels like harmony, a law that flies in all directions if we obey.

Sex is Red

Mother laid me
like a bag of little bottles
to bed.
Her hands were gifts
that filled me with small colours.

Now, lover,
you lie with me hard,
desperate for breath and my touch:
you want to see yourself in the broken glass

bloodied,
prismatic with the span of years,
pushing up
through my skin.

Try a Younger Man

Lately woman's way
is to younger lovers. It is natural
you have your revenge.
So go ahead, try the
turbine howling love of juveniles. Do so, but recall
my love is a morning's woods,
sap sensate but still.
Moss hums close to earth while head high
a red bird calls in flat-minor, simple.

Go, forget me,
try a tango with Ramone, follow
his cashier's wink and testosteronic bagging of cukes.
Just know that, when we touch, you remember yourself.
Mine is the seduction of empty space, warm brandy, talk.
A dusty history, opened along a strong spine.
When we touch, we hear Ramone's roar in the alley.
When we touch, the stars are cleaned of irony.
When we touch, we make a playground.
At the fence, the Ramones buck and lurch and cry.

Or try Vince. He will finger your confusion
with a maxim, binding time and mystery
as you grope your cheapest route out of
hard and shiny clothing.
Recall my love is a heron's walk, poise on ancient stilts,
and your love is the flashing of minnows.

Unlike young Jon, I hate *I Ching*, cards and dice games
unless they are played upon an altar.
I still have this love of pencils. So, go.
Take with you, facts.
When we touch, we kindle not the flame
but the growing space around it.
When we touch, children wake once quickly
and settle back.
When we touch, the howlings are made mute,
in the shapelessness
of our loving.

Admit it all comes down to winter shopping

You said we should be actors
to all of this—
players on the concrete,
orators in the snow.

I said—
Life is the empty barrel.
We must take the gaudy swandive
through the air to the very bottom,
bounce once, find each other's arms
and then die.

Today our minds are so full of food
we can hardly walk down aisles
of bright, attentive cans in rows.
Dead tired of each other's arms,
we push one more cartful
of bored meat,
hissing greens,
stupidly loud fruit.

We feel better after we've paid
and brought something of this other world
home with us.

Sex might not be so red

Sex might not be red
nor even a question of deep sea green, solar purple.
As I cycle the sunlit road,
the morning a robe I wear, fluttering behind,
sex is forgotten, a drained bottle,
or, more rightly, a single seed
—cold, mute, tiny-assed—
seated alone near my dark base of spine.

Pedalling, I hardly care. Look:
the day is bright, women step, gulls question mark the sky!
Whitman's crazy ghost of joy hangs in old men's faces. Today
they can't help it, their tomorrow
burned worlds away by this day's roaring colour.
Behind windshields, even the rush-hour barons settle back,
defeated, their fire smoldering to beige. They sigh,
snap on radios, and cycling curbside past the many stations,
I fancy it's me tuning a dial.

I stop, dismount, lock up, unband my trouser leg and
go in to buy an Italian vanilla cone.
You are forgotten. So, too,
the Laura of my red dreams.
Mother is, ambition is, the straining hyacinths that
blossom and tongue and seed: forgotten.
Hot pavement, my quietly flared nostrils, a cone. The robed day.
Sex cannot approach the sun.
The razor under my spine only forays so far.

Love from the urban basement sky

I am a man
city-made

Here I be
not over there

Watch my eyes
balletic for reasons
in the night

I am an art rat
modern, poor
but poolside

Come to me you

Come closer
your eyes alive with
the sugar of the street
I could cut them like strawberries
and lose no drops

I know
the city is lit for dark reasons
the lovers' pose is pain
art twists
and I can tongue your eyes
up

Finding

Water to water
as through sand, we meet.
Our newness buries the tomb.

Nearer to you than
blood to bones
dust in teacups
our skulls click in nervous kisses.

We lay new stones.

Loners

Don't talk to loners, she told him, angling a voice through the party noise. *Don't trust them. Like rivers hide salmon heavy with spawn, up their sleeves loners hide tricks.* He listened to her. *Loners. They aren't necessarily smart. At childhood a snap in the stomach does it.* Rising noise pushed them closer. *Don't trust anyone who flees the muddiness of friends. Her voice is unchecked, her madness nearly perfect. Her face treats you to all kinds of hors d'oeuvres. She knows your pulse without touching.* Ice tricked around in her glass, a child's tinkle-sound gone somehow sinister. *Dangerous to talk to a soloist. Her soul is burned from too much scrutiny. She will hunt over your head for exits. The bells of her eyes call with hunger you'll never fill. Deadly to love a loner,* she told him, *deadly to love us at all.* Edging away from her he backed into the wall. His shoulder hit the light switch. She stopped, spilled ice, startled by his eyes, seeing them for the first time, the bells there, louder than hers.

Three Contemporary Poems

1.

I ask you once more to join me
and explore the bed,
see if we find some urge there:
a thick red parrot
to trick us out of boredom again.

2.

You say, All babies become old men. And when
they die they scream like babies.
This should trick me into something, a new way of being.
But it does nothing. Nothing. And is it
even true? I'll phone someone and ask.

3.

At a 10 cent movie my dad said he saw an only child fall screaming
in sacrifice to the sun, cracking a chain of ancestry.
I don't know if I believe him.
Anyway, after sex with you, sundown.
This rolling rips the light off the world.
Old Sol, it seems, is angry,
peeling the last mysteries
away.

Christmas in Europe, Then Goodbye

Your brand of smile
calls to mind our past
the way mandarin oranges and gifts
make me see childhood Christmas.
Your visitations have grown darker.
Your touch fatal now
as a dimming candle: the ache deepens
like the soft close of light.

Let's talk true: we've seen the grey
borders of each other; it's no longer
morning; your body and smile are only knowing,
which is the decay of hope:
            decadence the natural
            scarring kiss
            time gives to anything gold or
            innocent as a holiday angel.

Our flight abroad,
our plotted rejuvenation in the ornate shells
of ancestors' culture—the graceful ashes
of a grander death—has told us the story
of ourselves:
            the historic smell of sex, our
            urbanity, our colours fading
            the wrong way, into canvas.
            Your black forest brambles, manicured,
            my spires, pocked.
            Your eyes are protected
            behind gallery glass.

It's a tired joy, this
birth of a night.
Much better the heralding of memory:
the young citrus of your mouth,
strokes of passion's wet and candied pigment,
the Yule of lust's toys.

Lunar Eclipse, Lighthouse Park

Sometimes the moon hides in earth's shadow,
unseen. This forces us to walk in darkness tonight.
Our feet wake to see the rocks.

A beacon sweeps, lights you up. Your cool face is all
I glimpse of a heart I cannot touch. I remember
that sun's light is safe for our eyes only when it comes
off the soft mirror of the moon. Fear of blindness
blocks the view a true heart would give.

We do our best to make connections.
We can lift a face to the shadowed moon and feel,
on our back, the sun shining through a world of rock.
Light searches for the moon, for your heart,
to illuminate.

II.
SEX BY NUMBERS

#1

I told you I was born
while falling to earth
out of a hole in the side of a mountain.
You say you were born in a dope shed
in riverfront Koohinoor
and died and were revived three times:
once by the smell of a monkey's haunch,
once by opium,
once by intimations of my face.

We make up stories,
then we make love
on the stories.

#2

We drop down from the hike
to the parking lot. Head swelling hot,
hotter because icy waters rush
just below.

The sun is absolute triumph
on your face.
Behind you, the mountain, behind that
the oven of solar purple.
Sweat erodes the dust on your cheeks,
rivulets let tiny white hairs
rise up and glisten.

You smile at my staring.
My tongue goes out
to taste the salt rivers
between your teeth.

#3

At least five of your looks
vaguely frighten people.
I see one and think,
there it is, your father's look.
Another when you bullied
your sister off a doughnut.
And there, a time
you must have said no
in a back seat.
Now in dawn light
I see you born again
mechanically, dreaming—
small muscles in your face
trying themselves
in amniotic fluid.

#4

The red rose is shut
and the lark is sober.

Like Epictetus
you are a slave
to the child killer,
the labyrinthine castle,
the drunken ruse of masks.

A lame emperor has said
your time is tied. The stones are set.

Softly, please, tell me
the best in your song
will unwind knots of terror.

#5

Union is a profession.

It is also a larger-than-life
picnic with you
—surprising hills—
the day hanging by a thread
of a mood
which may or may not
accommodate
the weather.

#6

In times of war carry a light bed:
Didn't you hint this the time
you held that heavy grudge for months?
You almost lost me then.
Each night, asleep, without
your real weight beside me
I had to float up
to find my first dream of you
and I was almost gone.

#7

You feel sick.
The full moon is all yours.

You get in a car and it drives you by
a nun trailing blood
past a grinning man selling
a dead dog on a string.

In your stomach
a porcelain doll head rolls slowly
as the moon turns its light.

#8

Hadn't seen her in moons. I phone.
After the machine beeps
I ask it: Want to come over,
try my new down quilt?
She was listening the whole time,
calls back, says, "Hey, I'm there."
Now, miles apart again,
voices extinct,
phones put down like old bones,
I pause in time,
steadied by a foretaste
of the cold season
in a cave, under fur.
The warmth of a thick
shared skin.

#9

You are staring into
3 a.m. coffee
trying to rediscover sugar.
Cannot recapture
crystalline islands
which were once your brace, your feet,
your milk and cookie retrospection.
Afterschool dollandTV
a kiss without doubt
belief without your
3 a.m.
web of brains.

#10

Fishing all day till
at last a cod in the bilge,
big-eyed, gulping. Conceived.
You scrutinized our dying dinner, eyeing
its tired final lifting of fins.
On the edge of guilt,
you took my hand, said
"My hero."
Something that shocks me about you
is your selfishness: unashamed.

We cooked it whole, Chinese style.
At meal's end, trailing a clean spine,
its big head makes
a bronze-eyed centerpiece.
You say, "It sees its murderer."

Knifing you in words, here,
my selfishness is slicker,
lidded.

#11

We've made our love a mountain
to be climbed.
Me, stopping to level my sandal at a pebble
in your path
and you, holding back branches that would whip
my eyes if you let go.
Trying this slope
we have to help each other.

But you've seen me, needing
a hand up, fall.
You were careless
or maybe you pushed.
Listen: they are both your same mistake.
And I never fail to look up to you
flicking mad rocks
from the top of our mountain.

#12

You say you've become an empty house
so thieves like me
find nothing to steal.

My first job is clear: furnish
our sturdy comfort.
A loveseat maybe, and carpets
woven by us.
In a hearth of lucky, found stones,
we'll fill our house
with fire.

#13

I say that it's a pendulum,
hard to divine, swinging
from love secular to sacred and back.
That love is complicated
by this drift from
urge to urge.

You say
love has no such map.
Only that one day we might find ourselves
standing nimbly on a hill, eye to eye,
sensing there's a fast baby in the bushes,
not yet conceived by us,
behind us,
blowing bubbles into our weightless hearts.

#14

Your book is closed tight.
Let a wind beyond words
blow music
on your skin tonight.

Glory
to you not charmed
by fragrant turn of phrase:
those prettiest of bells
that bind
wild arias

#15

Even drunk in a bar you insist
on driving all blames into yourself.
It's this bad: a fight breaks out
at another table and you think
it's your fault.
I watch your face closely then
and I do see
signs of the goddess.
Is dumb goodness enough, I wonder,
dumbly watching you sip beer and work
to descend on the barroom in mists of grace.

#16

I search her contradictions
like picking eyelashes out of my eye.
She wears a fur stole
made out of dead
agony.

She looks beautiful in it,
because she makes it look alive.

#17

sometimes, and I mean it lover
bitch, witch, evil evil bitch,
you lodge in my stomach.
you are the bursts of pain that
stretch the bounds of pain and
someday, I mean it, I'll
do you right
pain.

Will we all
laugh at this oddest loving
when we're well past death or
have you burned
oh have you burned out
our eternal eyes?

#18

I'm sick of this.
The sex of these words is grey.

There, good, I've let my heart
out of the bag.
Here it is, black,
an eye in the dark,
dilating

hoping the silence
at poem's end
attracts
unspeakable
colours.

#19

Let me add to everything I say:

Speech is a dumb
jumping rat, felt
first in the chest, up
the throat, then
too fast out the mouth, on feet,
while a tail slides long,
leaves hair, the wrong spice,
sibilance,
and the wish for a better
animal.

#20

You hunger
over glue pots
trying to make things
connect.

You punctuate,
plan.
And days go by,
anyway, your ladder
in pieces.

But this broken air
has a way of widening—
a mouth
with god-whole appetite.

Be food

#21

Are you leaving me a little at a time?
I dreamed you and I watched from bed as
moths, thicker than snow,
fell out from the ceiling
and fluttered to the floor, a two-foot deep
carpet. Their thousands of wings working
was the sound of thoughts rushing to the eyes
from the back of the brain.
You jumped from the bed and danced
in them, arms flung, jaw hanging, breathless.
The moths not crushed
don't know you stomp among them.
The rush of wings continues.

#22

I sometimes imagine you bald.
Odd of me, I know, your
hair being so fiery and fine.
I do it because I wonder how fixed I am
to the surface of you, the mere.
So next I remove your lips, your lashes.
I laugh, pulling off your nose,
your breasts and the rest of your body.
I leave the eyes for last, and when I expunge
them (a draining of two emerald lakes)
it seems you are left dimensionless.
Until I build you again.
As I add one thigh, an elbow tip, an eye,
the peculiarity of shoulder, your stride
in certain moods, then your lips, your nose,
I see it is not me doing the building.
As if something invisibly perfect
had opened secret hinges
to let light fall on its planes,
you come into view. You arrive
to my eyes from the centre of yourself;
you grow so wonderfully.
It confuses me now
how you decide when to cut your hair
or when to let it grow.

#23

I found an eagle half-buried in the sand
    the night was so cold
the bird could not properly rot

I found you drunk, half-naked in the sand
    the night was so cold
my fingers would not work

#24

A daytime downtown reconnaissance.
I say the busyness in these buildings
is empty as a glass dream.

Look at it again, you say, and
point to it shifting in women's dresses and
knotted at men's necks; you
taste its snap in the bubbles of
the hamburger we chew,
laugh at its heat coming off the gold in
Birk's window; find it, you claim,
not in the movie, but between the frames
of all that mechanical loving.

I ask you what it is, exactly. You say
it's everything
we could possibly
desire.

III.

INVITING BLINDNESS

One More Anti Ghazal Ghazal

I'm unsure as west coast snow what a ghazal really
is. Is it just a coy leap across this made up

space? Then, damn, it finds the ready enemy
in a man who lacks born logic-ear for line

breaks: me. I hate this then as I hate petty
politicians who do the fake Aeolian fuck-

step with words and laws binding the poetry of our lives.
You though, love, all but petty, look in your mirror

to see Leda wipe the muse off her loins and
wonder if her coming art will be in some

verse form, or a mind pigmenting mutely,
or in a simply more accurate pain. Never knowing,

you chose this. Oh, what to do with seeds!
I see I'm onto an old argument that form, any old

form, is a grid of prisoning, word wind turned gird stone,
while you, sad love, meet me half-way, wary in your

genius of sound's marriage to silence, your
bloodfear that no form is insanity's very bonelessness.

Here. No tricks. Half way seems right. For doesn't
the heart of the heart sutra say, "form is emptiness,

emptiness also is form"? Which means only maybe
merely that you damn well better look before you

fool around. Oh, lonely heart we've never met
but I believe I've been within your Morningside house

where I cringed in its knowing sadness, its
sense and non-sense spidered into concentric rings. I

smiled, closed my eyes, opened wide and pushed my best
out my pores for you. Though a novice at good

ness, I do try. Did you taste a trace of optimism
when you next pulled your fridge door and cracked an

empty egg? A tiny dancer's fluid rise? A gap in the air of
your bright kitchen? The smell of a harsh bird flying invisibly

away? I want the back of your head and shoulders to be
porcelain cool, the rilling of your basin to sound fresh

again, unutterable: words, after all, our wormy umbilical
to both paper space and our passing, oh our passing

time. You are older than me, lover. So, pained. Yet
wiser I see, your voice prismatic in the lamby

Saltspring mist, the sludge of an ebbing Ganges, the
bad viscous wordings of so many hard shoe wind

bag poets in whose number I do sometimes take
my place. Binding song, hooded monks chant

the apocalypse by rote. Gothic spires poke and
spurt dry at the womb of impossible freedom, the

sky. Soft lover, my leaping out of tight haunches, my
shy flight out of form reminds me of those first brave space

walks. Find: a cool moon. Sliding down Diana's nape,
rolling off her back, down, ah, *alive!* So artificial,

this.

It's Like

It's like discovering after so many years that around
all normal moods are *millions of emerald spangles*
fluttering like aspen leaves it's like watching the
grocery store clerk the one with the bad breath
turn luminous it's like Ezra Pound as a young man
licking his egg dish clean it's like ripping the
cold chain of bladder stomach spleen from a fish
to know the perfect cadence of your own hunger
it's like Allen Ginsberg meeting Roy Rogers who
bow and sing together in mutual shyness it's like
taming a coy flying horse with *a single green feather*
it's like blowing your nose *very properly and hard*
to free it of mucus gone solid *job done* it's like
spending your life's money on a circus ride called
All Alone

Mahayana

Like everything
from daydreams to dying, good lord
it's the urgent matter
of how to quick, help
slow it
up.

Let the horizon fall
from the moon.
The blood bugles
softly.
A tan flower
set upon a stream
tumbles around and down the current,
shaking off all doubt.
We arrive at the sea

as real, so to speak,
as meat
presented to lips:
bloody and
outrageously generous. We're safe
finding humour in the constant
dying.

See the boat, the
golden boat.
Let us loose our weapons
and with careful steps get on it.
When we meet the people here, warriors
   —not in the way of Homer; rather
    in the nature of tigers who chase us
    only to reveal our fear—
together we will drag rope, raise the sail
to catch the wind that pulls away
all directions
at once.

Texada Quarry

On this island I stand, booted and armed
to sweep away bark and earth,
bare the stone pure
for drillers and cutters and wedge hoes:
long days, many shapes of knife
to pare the rind of an island apple.

One iron, company hand
(but guided by human ephemera)
chips at the north tip of island stone,
doles out blocks, chunks, truck-sized squares
to bidders who with like-eyed tourists
ferry over in bulk. So Texada
is barged to town
and cut down, down again,
dope dealers splitting our core
into city dreams of exacto-brick
country-style hearth,
kids around it, warm
sanded rock mother.

One sunset Friday I saw the Comox jets practise bombing
these western waters and dreamed
how fast
the island rock called Texada,
the neat hearth of embracing mountains,
the warm children,
could be blasted, so clean
so small,
stone and clay shaped to fit the heavens
(but stone is birdlike for seconds only)
then fall and settle on our eternally
bald island globe.

Or we can chip it
by hand.

Living, Alone

—for D. Hayes

The slow drive to dusk moves heavily
from sight to mind, a recognition
of the sky's infidelity. Now into my own hands
falls the dying pattern of day.
Finished.
I walk to the shed, flick the axe inside,
and my gloves, hat, boots,
then run in my socks to the cabin,
feet surprised by dew that's not quite ice.
I am led to one drink, two,
to staring out the window at tomorrow's chopping
till the darkness
reveals my face on the pane.
Smile.
With one oil lamp
and a tough radio
I tune the brightest, loudest city known
to any lone man.
I sledge a spike into night,
tap my foot,
and dance on the wooden skull of the world.

The Fisherman

Our star is hot on board this middle-of-nowhere sea.
Hunting land, the air expands.

And there, hanging 16 herring on 16 hooks
the Indian lays a string of silver bait beads.
He jerks, stops, quick looks down
at the sense of something
in this deep, black mirror.

A still nowhere water shows him nothing.
Sees nothing.
He hears, smells—nothing.

When, sudden, his face is wild, tender
and all is so perfect
he leaps into all of it,
hovers there, in something like abundance,
under the sun, out of air
spread-eagle like a star.

He shouts songs below the wooden hull.
Sounding, booming the water-world drum.

And stops there, laughs
at a certain picture he gets
of 16 salmon
hanging below,
silver nuggets, round mouths, eyes
suspended in the coming magic.

The Junior Bazaar in Cairo

My favourite way of getting to sleep at night
is to dream the Junior Bazaar in Cairo.
Sheiks in sheets, brown and young,
their camels are small mountain ranges
behind every man, a warmth of caramel
moves on a tether, stretching to his hand.

Boys juggle by.
Girls glide in pairs, eyes wide enough
to share secrets wider than the whole world around them.
Men haggle at a bad price
with slack-face merchants sojourned behind thin boards,
greedy, and so close to unwholesome death
here in Cairo.

But, quartered in my bed
in Canada, the tough green
bushes, the rocks, snow, and wood,
and cement streets and houses with off-pink
liberal families inside,
and Toronto on TV, and politics,
French and English
dogs, and cold sunsets,
cloy of Lighthouse Park like the best Canadian postcard.
I am lost, deceived
unless I get to Cairo.
Deceived at work,
deceived on weekends at the flimsy beach.
Tricked in daycare centres, teased by *nouveau* décor,
flowers and faces painted *nicely*,
where long-haired, limp-faced women tend the children
Canadians.

Laughed at in local theatre,
pursued, possessed, bedeviled by
the real picture, on American TV—
the crafty, nonsensical poison.
Living so white
they try to get to Cairo this way:
deadwing flits to my bazaar.

I think of this in bed, my tongue on her body,
going for the rough spots, taking me closer
to the dinkled lights strung over my Cairo bazaar.
It all fades.
Driving to work, in billboards
the models' eyes wink faintly Egyptian,
tickling the world's ear with the Junior Bazaar.
But it fades: we are so white.

Not like when I bed down
at the longest stop-light in the world
and leap away
into where desert heat steams the Cairo pudding:
where the priests are green, green with blue beaks so
crazy
like the white Ibis
with yellow feet that dangle when it flies,
knocking at the knees,
chattering to all good-fearing merchants,
where *all* gods sing from the Cabala bush
in deepest Arabic
with song-like marbles rolling off a bell.

No cages here, in this bazaar, where
we can move where we are wanted most, and sing.

Awakening

—for Hugh

the log upon which the dog sleeps
                        is a marvellous log

brutes do not know that years ago
a man sat magic at a tree's foot
                        and entered it

see the dog rise, and stretch
                and smile
lips tight on set teeth

his eyes go only where they want

the log waits

Gifts

At noon he feeds his goldfish. It is the closest they come to happiness, though he doubts gratitude. At 3 a nod at the corner with the wheelchair neighbour gives him a sense of his own health, and luck. At 4 a sudden rainstorm puts the wild worm-and-pavement smell in his nose for a while. Then it is dark and streetlights come on all around. Who downtown has done this? At 6 the News gives him a taste of Middle East rage then takes it away for commercial time, when he is given the photographic beauty of well-poured beer. Next he is allowed to share in the puffy stitched face of a six-yr-old victim of a stray dog, or maybe a rare Eastern Cougar! Dinner puts hot butter and pasta and meat in his middle which feels nearly gone by Sports, where he is granted statistics of physical achievement he knows involve vast sums of money for certain gifted people. As a sort of bonus for everyone, the anchorman offers a News Flash: Edmonton has been presented with a surprise tornado! There are suspected dead; eye-witnesses are excited as kids at Christmas. By 8 the brandy has unfurled its comforter behind his eyes and all offerings are fuzzier, more amiable. Out his window, framed, the moon again, hinting its story that feels both old and new, and looks like a mirror, and sounds like language he might someday learn but hasn't yet. He treats himself to more brandy, feels the need to receive as a shield that precipitous gift, irony, in order to close his eyes on the night again, in order to once more refuse the question, who is bestowing all of this upon him, and why.

Inviting Blindness

To mate, stuck together
and flying four wings strong,
the Arizona black bee
shoots straight up
at the sun.

Not to draw cheap analogies but
Icarus did this lonely and alone.
And so much for intelligence: bees know the sun
as a brightness a short buzz away.
Lover, let's not take for sacred
a blind surge
or see meaning in mindless binding.

But picture: you and me at our wildest
joining
in furious harmony
an impossible chasm
of sky

Kairos Time

—for Lise, April 5, 1987

To put it simply:
you are born
the night the father
dies.

This wind is intent.
This night, intended.

The stars are brightest in years,
and the call goes out, in a language
of mouths larger than galaxies.

Their breath
allows exchange
of souls.

A Heaven

why's it that rummies
have the ugliest noses?

pocked or,
convexly,
warty

seems it's not just the booze
but a general release
of the status quo
propping the face:
full freedom from
flesh-pride

seems there's almost a humour here
so close to
a delirious death
so close
to salvation—
down
secret
in those urinal
hospitals:
men who share
the common poison
thrash in fear of the God of
wild lights
coming too fresh
off the wet, antiseptic floor

More Sex is Red

Perhaps the world wars
because sex is red.

Is this right, dear?
Can I compare my hunger for you
to others' primal pains:
   they've never met their one and only god
   yet insist to the death
   He's a better Man than any One
   you can come up with;
   or Manifest Destiny: the lost pregnant land,
   the vast black-earth delta from before
   the snake found knowledge,
   or Jesus just a piece of good garden
   on the stupid neighbour's side of the fence
—anything we don't have but want, any
scarlet lusty illusion at all.

I will not say sex is
a red white and blue bully—
that is cheap, hardly fair
and in the end sex is simpler,
a single colour, a primary
demand that the soft skin of your inner leg
allows my tongue and no other.
And a demand to taste the summer figs again

as a free man in Damascus.
And I demand your wayward heart stop,
turn, see me, stay.
The pews of South Carolina creak
with sex-swollen people, sufferers like me,
backs erect, liquid eyes up and
bursting with lusty glory from
a taste of what isn't there and
a faith that demands
nothing less than
you.

The Sex of One World

1

Along the main hot road
I pedal out of summer into rumours of winter,
sweep past the glint of glass
from last night's bottle fights,
smell the old oil in the gears
between my feet,
see birds arking the periphery of my fast head
or hear them hiding in trees.
When they cry out up close
their whole small body flexes like a heart.
Is what we call birdsong—a human-pleasing
air, curved and tuned
by a wee throat—just a sexyell,
loud as the dumb bird
can do it?

If I stop more than a minute I smell sun on my skin.
So, off again, curb-launch,
car, honk, falling wino, I'm too fast
to help in the deadly season—
we tend to bike the main road with head down,
pumping, cycle past that store sidewalk rack,
the war on page one there—
pedal by it hard,
glide now and lift a hand to pick the celery string
in my teeth that's bugged me all day
on and off, according to the simple law of
one thing at a time—one word per object,
one line per breath, one war per tabloid inch,
one hunger for each heart beating.

2

It's a grand tarnished house
where we do live. Lawns wild
with spray—its groundskeeper's
insane vandals.
We try to cycle away, sensing
cancers most inopportune, like cauliflowers
billowing out of friction.
Trying not to see through walls, we pass squat banks,
and armoured car jams, and faculties lounging, and
Tetris screens, and board room trusts
fixing the next junior style. The bleakest
language is bureaucratic.
Out of here, god, out of here, it should be
the countryside by now, but here we are
at the bank again.

I imagine my blood swelling with final panic
of hope and fear, and I take out my heart savings and
strap huge sacks of flour to my back
and cycle long miles up
to a perch at the very summit. You're here too;
there are so many of us, it's surprising;
some of us are ugly and not too smart and seemingly
weak, but we gaze out, and our fast doughy hands
make tortillas, chapatis, kaiser rolls, pita,
Russian black rye and matzo and Wonder Bread
in a plea for good common peace.
It begins to rain, signalling futility
or at least years and years soggy work baking,
each raindrop an omen

of the next raindrop,
each a strophe of some mute wisdom perhaps,
a reminder that we breathe until we die.

3
Below, on a rising black mountain
of their own making,
bad boys bare their sex in the face
of what they see to be a bad world.
They're seething. It's only natural.
They will do it again, say the clouds,
reshaping like a wringing of hands
      —it's old Whitman's crazy voice, Whitman
        who tended the screaming blue and bloody rows
        of civil war boys until his own blood battled
        his brain and killed his body and released
        his old voice up into the clouds at the summit—

We bake the boys a cream cake large enough
to fill them and ease their sleep.

And coast down from the summit
leaning into switchbacks
with the heavy glide of an albatross.
My sweat blows cold in such descending,
my song is blown back down my throat.
I muse on death and how
warm life changes to ice in its quick drop.
Reaching bottom I buy a PorkyHot on a Bun

at the old Ramona Deli in the flexed heart of town
from a fat European who every day
talks of war and weather with friends
and fights his own battle with the good food
he sells to people like me
cycling by.